ne

ADVENTUS

Sue Vickerman

naked eye

Naked Eye Publishing

© Sue Vickerman 2017

All rights reserved

Book design and typesetting by Naked Eye

ISBN-13: 9781910981054

www.nakedeyepublishing.co.uk

Acknowledgements

Thanks are due to poets Jennifer Copley, Jean Stevens, Jean Harrison and Kim Moore for their comments on some of these poems, also to Naked Eye managing director Michael Kilyon for his superhuman patience, and as always to Alison Marshall for fulfilling the role of muse.

The cover illustration is a linocut by artist printmaker Helen Peyton from a series of four entitled Christmas. One of these has been purchased by the Victoria and Albert Museum in London for its permanent collection. Helen Peyton's works are exhibited at the Royal Academy, the Scottish Academy and Leeds City Art Gallery, and are collected all over the world. She is based in the Yorkshire Dales in England. *helenpeyton.com*

Versions of a few of these poems have appeared in previously published poetry collections by Sue Vickerman, including some under the pseudonym of her created character 'Suki'.

Contents

The coming 11
The ends 13
A hearth in wintry weather 14
A better life 16
Life and death in the Loire Valley 18
The last of me 19
Popular piety 20
Gift 21
Christmas tree 22
The end of love 24
The thing not said 25
The last keepers 26
How Christa changed everything 27
The Siege of Bethlehem 28
No room 30
…spent it at the cottage in Withernsea 32
The three wise men 33
Not snowing but raining 34
Canal Christmas 35
The Festival of Nine Lessons and Carols from King's College Cambridge 37
Jesus's big sister 38
Son 40
December 23rd 41
December 24th 42
New Year's Eve 45
Notes 47

1
The coming
Britain's decision to leave the European Union in 2016 was influenced by fears propagated by the Leave campaign of an uncontrollable deluge of refugees.

It starts as a tranquil Advent morning.
The church's bell. I put Radio 4 on.
Fusty cottage bed smell. My small skylight an
old-style grey-scale grainy screen, sleety rain
flitting across it, a bit of sun due later
so I rise, breakfast, thinking to
leave behind the troubling headlines and
walk on the fell's dry-stone-wall-bevelled loveliness -
stacked-up rocks that go back centuries,
luscious mosses that go back millenia,
sleet, rain, sleet, now slithery heather,
now tactile lichen-laced granity crags,
grey-green meadow where my boots leave
soft scoop-shapes on sheep-tracks
that peter out and restart and randomly
meet the upper path where suddenly, a dark thing
on the fell-top frightens me, profiled, dalek-like…

What if another and another appear on the
brittle skyline? What if they come pouring over
our northern hills like sheep being driven down,
til this bench with a plaque marking Bob Dugdale's
beloved look-out point turns to a mucky pit
messed up with detritus - plastic bottles, baby wipes,
a dirty dolly, a dummy, litter, piss, shit?
What if they pour down the fell, soiling it while
calling out, stumbling, pushing, tripping, falling -
then set up stall in the mud and try to cook?
Where's this black-bearded man from? Palms

capping the skulls of two lost-looking children,
dirt-smeared, tear-stained, blood, sweat, snot.
What if they come and come and... And a mother's
yelling at a youth like our Emma would with Andrew
what must be *stop, stop, stop,* as his desperate
leap to get over the beck's lethal tumult fails.

2
The ends

The first end happened
on the way to the therapist
when we said in the car
what we were going there to say

But it didn't end there. Was the end when I got practical -
where should I move to? Since
I couldn't by myself afford this house's rental -
but she stalled, seemed not quite ready yet

or was the real end telling our parents at Christmas that
although our gifts were *from* us both
and the gifts we were receiving were *to* us both
We were no longer *together*

though technically still under the same roof,
though still the best of friends although it had ended
(though we didn't go into details,
the silences, her resentment, our separate beds)

and the new year started but she didn't move on
so I moved on, I got my own place and
moved on but for god's sake she moved on with me
because she seemed not quite ready yet

so there we were, separated but rubbing together
in my tiny place, it was uncomfortable and I wanted it to end,
when is it going to end, *look it's the end Annabel,*
and by the end it was not amicable.

3
A hearth in wintry weather

To think Cecily roller-skated in this very quadrangle
that's now a car-park: big heavy pre-war skates
amid this compound's villas, Ju Lu Road.
Herbaceous borders, privet live with snakes,
redbrick, English roses, railings. Shanghai 1936.

It's tarmaced now, parked up with Bentleys, black flex
laxly looped along the trees delivering internet
to that coffee outlet where a child in gingham skated,
blazer flung off after jostling in a rickshaw
from the cathedral school down Huashan Road -

wicker chairs scattered about, barrista
in spectacles, chrome pipe hissing milk out,
pretty girls in thigh-boots drinking lattes
taking selfies, laughing like Cecily did
crashing into a plant-pot… While in a Cotswold town

that child, now ninety-nine, is in the Lion, after internment,
all that happened - repatriation, Hampstead flat, offspring,
gîte in Lorraine, the accident, Prozac, breakdown
then top award, second husband, third; dog-breeding,
Wales and the legal battle, A-level in Norwegian

and now here, reflected in an age-speckled mirror
looking happy in candlelight with half-drunk pint,
snow flocking on the window, log fire roaring
as a fiddler flicks his pony-tail then starts a folksong
and trippers in raingear drink heritage ales, tapping along,

these typical locals, this friendly barmaid popping a
borrowed knitting pattern back into Cecily's rucksack
while Cecily claps, laughing like when she crashed into that pot,
as if none of it happened - near-starvation, addiction,
another affair, avalanche at Gaustablikk, that poodle craze -

because life is a hearth in wintry weather, nuisance bladder,
pay the milkman, read the paper, did I switch the cooker off,
Sudoku, Banbury cakes, Nurofen, Pot Noodle.

4
A better life
This poem owes its form to Alan Ginsberg whose 'American sentences' are poems of seventeen syllables in one long line, capturing a moment.

Someplace nice, English spik, house have faucet, my kids no get shot, not bomb.

Ten months *Aufnahmezentrum*, kids good in *deutsch*, I bad in *deutsch*, wife none.

Ramadan we don't eat in day, in night eat lot, but my wife don't want.

Nice apartment - three rooms, I like cook, people friendly, kids play *Fussball*.

My job is okay, make kebabs, get Euros to my wife, give her all.

I love cooking work - also in home, because my wife is *depressiv*.

Racists come for kebab, speak bad words in *deutsch*, my wise girl says forgive.

My wife is sick in mind, I am very worry, she wants to go back.

I say our country is fuck-up - think our kids - but she says she can't think.

My kids are at college now, strong in their minds not the same like mother.

I will open a fast food restaurant with Gary my new brother!

My girl qualified psychiatric, I did good as single parent.

My son says the American Dream stinks, he has politics talent.

I shave and feel young again but my boy grows a beard, don't ask me why.

My new wife is Renata - she speaks excellent English; so do I.

My son, my son, my son, what have you done, oh my god, my only son.

Renata left me, the apartment is cold, all the windows broken.

5
Life and death in the Loire Valley

Outside the brasserie, rattan chairs,
candles in jam-jars, me in my linen suit
skimming the newspaper over an espresso

while feathers float by from an eiderdown
hung on a balcony as tourists wander past -
floppy hats, skimpy frocks on sexy hips;
as smoke from a grill in a garden drifts over,
cutlets sizzling, pool water dazzling and
dancing. Life would be as perfect as this

if the young mum on the front page
had not swallowed the fatal pills but instead,
on this golden evening, could have slid
shimmering out of that pool -
the luscious drag on her olive limbs -
like another young mother just did.

You could have been her - yes, rubbing
your child dry, pulling on a sun-dress,
passing bread round, having a laugh,
me knocking the kid's ball back, sipping
an espresso after sweating at the office,
savouring this day's completeness -

a single minute - coffee aroma, beautiful girls
and beyond these verdant hills
the sea azure, exquisite.

6
The last of me

One rickety chair, two plants long-dead
on the mantelpiece, solitaire laid out
three-quarters played, a crisp packet,
some crumbs on a plate, an eye of mould
in a pot of tea, the tab-end of my last cigarette.

You come to price the furniture, lift carpets,
fill plastic sacks with the fridge's contents,
my underwear, my worthless ornaments,
the stuff in the bathroom cabinet. Some things
fall to bits when moved - I could have told you that.

My keys must be deposited at the council offices
in office hours. Please do a final tour of the flat
once empty, take out the ash bucket, thank you,
that last sad floor-cloth can go, and leave it
just as it was before I ever lived here.

7
Popular piety
Inspired by Patricia Smith's not-just-for-kids acrostics.

Phoebe's M.Phil on child-abusing monks fed into her
  breakdown.
Oonagh, full-blown nun, twin of Pat-single-mum, is happily
  celibate.
Paul, now Bilal, converted after arriving in Batley by bus where
Uddin was tending his murdered brother's pop-up shrine in the
  terminus.
Lara Legs & Lips feels called as a Christian to service war
  veterans.
An Da's schooling in Shenyang instilled a need for
  regimentation while
Rudi's Kindertransport trauma instilled into him an acute
  sense...

Pat, giving up men for Lent, got dildos for herself and her nun-
  twin.
Ian, off his face on something, ran down so-called 'Bilal' in
  his Cortina.
Eli forsook his lover and started a forum for gays who repent of
  their sin.
Thomas has turned to mindfulness since his addiction and since
  leaving
Yvette, who has no truck with the load of crap that all these
  mugs believe in

                        except for her Jewish grandpa.

8
Gift

They're rebuilding our house after the bomb.
Our door's a real door now, not a curtain;
dirt floor boarded over - pitch pine planks,
distressed. They've put in plumbing.

On my first day they chat, showing me
how they've kept it simple: old-style phone,
retro bathroom-suite (though flush toilet),
wood-burning stove, reclaimed, original.

They're sorry about the missile
that took out our street - they're here
as ordinary civilians. They worry
for us. They want to be friends.

As cleaning jobs go, it's an okay one.
Our attic has become his gym.
There's a hobby room for her - she paints.
They've put nice lamps in

and glazed the windows. They had to,
she apologised, not being used to mosquitoes
like us natives. Out by the bins,
our corrugated lean-to, dismantled.

December. An inflatable Santa on a newly-
rolled-out lawn, and a gift: permission to
take back the lean-to that was our kitchen,
so long as we don't drag but lift it.

9
Christmas tree

And I'm waiting outside in the Fiat,
me thinking, another year, Craig in Asda
comparing tree specifications -

Craig who makes expert coffee, owns four bikes,
changes our sheets weekly, diligently wipes marks
off the laminate, de-lints coats, flosses, recycles -

when one of your acorns clops onto the windscreen

and I see the jagged star your torso's rising out of
cracking open the car-park's tarmac; you
towering over, wind-tossed, scattering jetsam

while lining the kerb stick-thin saplings
flutter, fairy-lights twinkling, flirtatious,
arms clacking up at you -

(Craig loading the boot with a three foot fir -
blue-black, fibre-optic, on offer - little-bummed
body in cycling shorts sliding into the seat cat-like)

and I want to be willowy! Join their girly party,
twigs in my knickers, be another in your long string
of rackety affairs, a lover in your harem...

Later, after a fish supper and sex with Craig
I say put it up then, I'm popping back to
Asda for dishwasher tablets, and slip away

and when he cycles over in the early hours
searching with his silly head-torch, he only sees
an oak tree; not, at your crux, my silhouette -

legs winding, fingers woven into the shaggy nest
between your thick thighs, my body limpetted
onto yours, adoring your cavernous darkness.

10
The end of love

Alone in a new way. Him sat down the other end
of the sofa, the counsellor's eyes exceedingly pain-filled
fixed on the dralon gap across which my twenty-six-
year-long lover won't reach, even though I am crying.

Have we each been alone all along without knowing?
A memory: grass tickling my upper back's
bare skin, little shreds of green
not smothered, no - pressing up into me eagerly.

Silly isn't it but he'd be ready now, he says,
if, in my birth canal, as then, if sperm were again
breast-stroking strongly through semen newly in me
on that sheet-white spring-skied English picnic afternoon,

my back pressed into our long narrow garden's
fresh Easter grass, my outline left like the flattened patch
we'd found on moorland after a sweet sun-bathing lamb
sprang up in front of us and ran…

Beyond the consultation room, uncertain hills;
a changing light that never would have worried me
before. But now, no hand is reaching out to reassure.
A feeling more acute than 'loved' is to be 'not loved'

and old
childless
insecure
damn you.

11
The thing not said
A ghazal¹

With so much still to say, you never said goodbye.
That Christmassy snow-day, you never said goodbye.

After our split but before our final parting,
your first staying-away, you never said goodbye;

even meeting to do the dividing: *take this* –
and you'd say *okay* – but you never said goodbye.

Leaving our joint-owned house, your terrier - my step-dog -
would lick me goodbye but you never said goodbye

though I patted farewell to the button-back chair
as your truck drove away. You never said goodbye.

Then in the station car-park, New Year's Day -
you heading for Calais - you never said goodbye,

me getting out of my car by coincidence,
surprised I said - *Hey!* - but you never said goodbye,

only – *Rain again!* - stepping in puddles, unseen –
Well, don't miss your train then, you never said goodbye,

though stations are a fitting scene, rough cheek on mine
tingling like a graze, but you never said goodbye,

just - *Jen* - and in your muscular-looking leather
jacket, walking away, you never said goodbye.

12
The last keepers
The Northern Lighthouse Board's automation programme, completed in 1998, brought to an end the era of resident keepers.

At Christmas a storm raged in from the sea
and entered the lighthouse, left our tree
decked with shells, hung with curls of kelp,
sea-creatures stuck all over like charms,
small driftwood sticks suspended
from its upstretched arms, up top a starfish.

We'd been shouting again, out on the cliffs, shouting
above the turbulence where the wreck lies hidden -
the sky looking volatile, fighting with itself
then knifed in two by a military jet -
when the wind got up and came right at us,
scraping skin raw, stopping us breathing,
biting into the skeletal finger of our house
until skulls of seabirds littered the bathroom,
bladderwrack slopped in the backs of cupboards,
pebbles lay scattered on carpets; meanwhile
in the stubbled mess of a close-cropped field
we went on shouting, not hearing.

In January I flung the tree from the headland.
At first it caught, the way a crampon snags
on rock, then tumbled down as you watched.
Later you salvaged more driftwood for kindling
but I could not burn the twisted pieces,
etched with wormholes, rotten, beautiful.

13
How Christa changed everything

And we reflect on our childhoods in Nazareth
before you got to where you are today,
when girl-fun was a donkey-ride to market,
flirting with your dad's apprentice carpenters,
girlifying our brothers' dens with curtains.
Mariam's falafel. Elizabeth's hand-knitted mittens.
Girl-talks on love, on saving the world, on being mums,
girl-talks about angels and how to become one

before my marriage and your raised consciousness,
my kids, your drivenness, the transwoman carpenter
whose case you fought, your guilt at her death sentence.
You've taken up the issue like it's your life's mission,
but tonight, reminiscing, swigging red wine
in the dunes, tell me you're not wistful for
the old Nazareth, before she brought notoriety
and all the visitors; for those simple girl-things.

14
The Siege of Bethlehem
Inspired by the 2002 occupation of Bethlehem by the Israeli Defence Forces in their effort to capture Palestinian militants.

O little card fallen off the rack in the stationery aisle,
how familiar are your stylised representations
of mud-built houses: flat-topped constructions,
half-tennis-ball domes, those untidy dwellings
like shoeboxes stacked on the saddle of that hill,
the impossible constellations of your night sky.
O little card on the supermarket floor
you get picked up then dropped again

    while, in a poor area depicted in one corner where
three camels stand waiting near a hoarding
ripped in two by the turret of a tank, a helicopter
is circling a warehouse with light shining out of it,
pointed at by the long prong of a star. And I wonder
how many are crammed in, taking refuge;
whether there are barricades of filing cabinets,
bloodstained carpets, windows shattered by rifle fire

yet still some normality: notes stuck on monitors,
ring marks from coffee cups, a sandwich, half-eaten,
the team leader's screen-saver showing her kitten,
as black smoke drifts over from the bomb
left in a manger, or was it a mule, explosive-laden.
O little town with so many mean rooms
where cigarettes and guns lie side by side on tables,
where pull-out deals are brokered then undone,

over here in the chilled area by the fish counter
they are setting up a grotto, the toy aisle
filling with children, check-outs humming,
the deli promoting profiteroles, Cliff Richard singing
while there, among the bombed-flat buildings
before you skid under a freezer, is an ambulance
stopped at a checkpoint, its driver staring at
lemon trees, intact, miraculous in the barren field.

15
No room
Luke 7:2

They come knocking. I know the look:
the jeans and hoodies, schoolgirl mums
with bairns in buggies, homeless teens
with hacking coughs pretending
they've got money in their pockets;
beggars, junkies, alcoholics, loners,
bloodshot eyes in sunken sockets,
failed asylum seekers on the run;
the unwashed couples, their bedding
in bundles, their stoned-looking mongrels,
their bad smell, bad skin, pierced tongues;
the lies they tell, the sob-stories
when we all know what the truth is.

Take this pair. Same tale every winter:
girl like a house-side in a blue burka,
teatowel on the head of the other, sandals
in this weather and a donkey in tow
instead of a dog. Strewth! Other cultures.
This must all be meaningless to them:
sea-front illuminations, big tree
on the roof of the Hilton, our neighbours'
inflatable snowman. No appreciation.
I point out my sign, tell them No Vacancies;
I say No room! No room! - not for your lot
at any rate - and close my door, and watch
from behind my curtains as they hesitate.

The telly announces how chilly
the day's been. Tonight it will be bitter.
Frost has winkled into my double glazing.
I knock on the glass, tell them Hop it!
until they trot back down my path at last
and clop along to the next guest-house.

16
...spent it at the cottage in Withernsea

but all there was was the usual tree,
its driftwood hangings, burnt-down candles,
dull cardboard stars, a couple of strings
of broken shells, a lack of glitter -

and abstract longings; how it used to be
love, peace, Jingle Bells, snow, warmth, light,
crowded settee, childish happiness, fights
over chocolate, paper hats, one long laugh

but all there was was a fridgeful of left-overs,
Radio 4's nostalgia trip through the last twelve months,
The Archers omnibus where Phil and Jill said
Christmas had never been better.

17
The three wise men

To cap it all it was cold. Really cold,
and rough terrain, and all of us old,
and nearly coming to blows over the route
through those dark dunes to get to the bairn,

and we were loaded up. So heavily loaded
and the camels weren't good. How they groaned
under the weight of all that gold. But we had a role,
and there is no record of us moaning,

nothing of three wise men with frost-bitten toes
missing strong brown Yorkshire tea
in that strong-brown-tea-forsaken desert
and nobbut camels' milk, no cows,

and no really boiling water, nor proper pot,
and blaming each other for who'd forgotten it
and as we plodded, read in the stars the laddie's fate -
what we each thought we could well foresee -

but disagreed on every time and every date,
and finally had to agree to disagree.

18
Not snowing but raining

When I left the house it was raining.
Not snowing but raining although this was Christmas Day.
I left you all in the house.
I left that house that life and went out, though it was raining.
The kind of person I am
all the fun going on in the house, I left it. In the rain.
Houseful. Children in-laws dogs

yet I ran out into the

because I couldn't

that house

d'you still

19
Canal Christmas
A prose poem[2]

At the carol service during While Shepherds Watched - still undecided about how best to get through the next forty-eight hours - I am re-living being Gabriel: the frock made of a sheet that I tripped on while climbing up the back of the crib-scene to get above the baby and open out my sheet-wings. How magical it all once was.

The vicar talks about protest, loneliness, corporate greed, his face up-lit by a candle. I don't know what righteousness means. Saviour I understand as a basic human need. When he reads about those who live in a land of deep darkness, I know that place. When he ends with the promised advent of the Prince of Peace, I want that man

but instead I meet up with you at the anti-capitalist encampment in Centenary Square. Bright snow has cleaned everything; sky glittery, incredible, behind Sheryl on her makeshift platform addressing passers-by about a better world. *We are you*, she cries out to the dark city, but only the two of us plus a homeless Polish builder smoking in front of the tents hear her, and it is anyway far too cold

so here I am, after all, on your houseboat parked in a canal basin, hanging lights round this cactus, putting out a stocking for a man who doesn't even do Christmas, who is off alcohol but I nonetheless open champagne

and in the morning you are embarrassed that I have filled you
such a big sock that spills everywhere, gift-wrapped packages
interspersed with little chocolate Santas although you're also
off sugar. I say - just a few bits, it's nothing, thinking, no sock
big enough for everything I want to give you out of guilt at
feeling so sad; you saying - I really love you; me saying - oh
Rowan, don't, and as we're having sex (all the little gifts
getting re-parcelled in duvet), as someone embarrassingly calls
out Merry Christmas from the towpath, my eyes are closed; I
may never come to this houseboat again

but, obliviously happy, you take me to the Festival of Political
Song at the anarchist squat where a reunited nineteen-eighties
women's chorus is singing new lyrics about menopause
symptoms as well as the old ones about men's inadequacies, till
a Marxist rocker I vaguely know takes over, his theme
exploitation: call-centre workers, cockle-pickers. He does a big
strum for the end of the socialist dream but grins as though
there is no greater thing on Christmas night than to play a guitar
on this podium on the second floor of a derelict woollen mill;
these women who are newly grandmothers, this man who sells
car parts; he, the boy in the playground who would pinch my
arm or ignore me altogether when I tried to play at fainting,
when all I wanted was to be saved.

20
The Festival of Nine Lessons and Carols from King's College Cambridge
A ghazal[1]
This famous Christmas Eve service, broadcast live on BBC1, tells the story of Christ's birth through carols and bible readings, commencing with the carol 'Once in Royal David's City', the first verse being sung solo by a boy chorister.

You love his quavering solo, mouth making tall 'o's;
the calm before tomorrow, mouth making tall 'o's,

how it cuts to a wavering candle, close-up,
then pans to choirboys in rows, mouths making tall 'o's

while your mother hands round bowls of dates and chocolates
and nuts, and comes and goes, our mouths making tall 'o's

as we belt out the carols, squashed on the old couch,
passing a tin of Roses, mouths making tall 'o's.

You love all the wrapping-up and unwrapping and
really wanting it to snow, mouths making tall 'o's,

the crowns got from Christmas crackers, tinsel haloes,
singing with family, closeness, mouths making tall 'o's,

til bickering breaks out when an old carol starts
that none of the children knows, mouths making tall 'o's

then Mum calls through *there's mince pies in the kitchen* and
suddenly everyone goes (mouths making tall 'o's) -

even the dog's gone. A bauble drops off. Peace - *Snow
on snow, sno-ow o-on snow,* mouths making tall 'o's -

and there's just you, our Sue, always the different one,
singing, alone, eyes closed, your mouth making tall 'o's.

21
Jesus's big sister

It's not in the bible, what he suffered
in the stable, poked at with a sharp straw -
his torn, sore mother too weak, Joseph
dealing with guests - that poor child
smothered nearly to death with false kisses.
What did it do to him, having hot wax
dripped on his cheek, his blanket set fire to?

The shepherd starts saying *All I've brought is*
but Big Sister snatches his lamb: I want that!
You take the brat. The scuffle wakes Jesus.
She stings his face with donkey-poo bullets
then spots a gift tucked into the manger.
Frankincense. She flings it everywhere, Joseph
laughing it off, putting the myrrh on a top shelf,
the kings nice about it - she has made a temple,
holy air, the first woman to honour him.
Take our word - they'll come in droves, beg
for his touch, clean his feet with their hair.
Big Sister gives them the finger.

And when her brother shines at theology
she snickers at the back mocking him,
smokes pot, flunks her catechism.
My brother thinks he's so good. Arsehole.
Down the souk Saturdays, she starts nicking

and at night, on the shared roof where they lie
on their mats beneath the stars, she spits
bad words at him - When you were born
I dropped out of our parents' orbit. Bastard -
he silent, she sneering into the dark -

you make me puke. Why love everyone?
People *hate* people like you.

Every good thing, she does a big yawn.
When it turns out he has healing gifts
she goes in the dunes with camel-men
then when his ministry takes off full-blown,
she steals his gold and elopes to Babylon.

What made him forgive so much sinning?
Why didn't he hate all females? His mum
for letting her bully him; that Mary Magdelene?
How come, right through, Jesus still loved women?

22
Son

I remember the turtle doves that morning,
the oxen they startled, dung piled in a corner,
a shepherd's crook jammed upright in the sand,
a lamb in the man's knapsack, straw prickling
in my underwear, Joseph batting his hand
at an insistent fly, and beyond the window
the momentary glitter of a snowflake like a star.

You don't hear this said, but I had it hard,
even with the heart-warming carol,
the lovely singing-voice of the angel whose face
was like a painting, the king who marvelled
at the music's quality in that glory-hole of a stable –
the same chap who brought the bitter perfume
and explained about anointing.

Don't get me wrong, I was grateful
for the presents cluttering the manger,
the swaddle hand-made in lace by another king,
words of adoration over and over again
and the peace, at the beginning;
so much goodwill and above all else above
all else, the first scent of my belovèd, still bloody.

But right from getting off that donkey to the
brutal end that I watched in person I tell you
I had it hard. In all the coverage, in version after version
the main thing got missed out, yet these myths
now thrive. They're not something I bother with,
only, I'm glad that his picture's still everywhere,
that people still wish him alive.

23
December 23rd

I woke up in a fog like flannelette,
came out of the crook of my elbow
thinking we were in England, seeing the milk-bottle blue
whiteness through the glass, the way sheets
would fill back yards up north -
remember that?

The train was at a halt.
The sign read *Idar-Oberstein*
in tall, bent script like piano fingers

and I glimpsed, below the famous cliffs, the town's outline
when the fog swished back then drew closed -
not pretty like the postcards, but caught off-guard
with that same feeling of emptiness lingering over
every place we'd stopped at.
Prob'ly nice in high season

I said, train slipping out of the station,
but I caught you in the double-glazing smiling
for no reason, smiling right through me so sadly.

24
December 24th

It is almost five. It is *Heiligabend*.
The forecast shows snow cartwheeling over Saarland.
The sun goes down on your cul-de-sac,
on your parents' small, well-tended garden.

Your yard is swept. Your steps are gritted.
Your mother's broom rests in an apple tree's elbow.
She hurries outdoors at the very last minute
to dead-head a rose.

Your father is on the point of lighting
the candles on a tree dug out of the Saar Basin
which, from the plane, glittered
like a Christmas card.

You have always told me how the waiting
was hard; was the best thing of all: how,
when the bells finally toll across the valley,
the whole village feels holy.

and then comes…

New Year's Eve

I remember the deathly silence afterwards,
how flat the land was, a scribble
of poplars, pencil-sketched bushes,
the blank look of a lake in December,
sky like a drawn-down blind
as wide and high as a Suffolk winter

but this was Zarrentin, six hours
before the end of the year;
a muddle of trees, a twisted puzzle
of a root, a leafless bush,
one last red berry in its claw like a pill,

a weekender from Hamburg
power-walking, shattering ice lids
from the tops of puddles; the special issue
dropped from his rucksack
as he sprinted into the distance
before I could call him back,

leaving me with the English prices,
tanks in a line, a lottery-winning family,
a child's distended belly, a soldier's grin

and the nakedness of a tree
lying where it fell beneath the weight
of disused nests, the rotting stomach
of a rowing boat dragged out of the lake
and upturned, the dried-blood smell
of mushrooms on carcasses

and still six hours: it wasn't over yet;
and the sharp, ugly phrases of ducks.

Notes

1. The ghazal is an ancient poetic form found in the Middle East and India, having its origins in Arabic poetry long before the birth of Islam. Ghazals are typically expressions of profound emotion, perhaps on the theme of love, often solemn or melancholic, sometimes set to music.

Structurally, a ghazal is made up of between five and fifteen couplets, its most distinctive characteristic being its refrain, which first occurs at the initial couplet's two line-endings, then is repeated at the ending of the second line of each further couplet. This repetition helps to create a bond with the audience, since it often elicits an eventual joining-in.

The form has two further rules: a recurring rhyme should appear throughout the poem in the second line of each couplet, preceding the end-of-line refrain; also, each line ought to have the same number of syllables, though in English-language ghazals (unlike in the form's original Eastern usage), there is no specified meter for these - which means it's easier to write one. So have a go! See contemporary British (Iranian heritage) poet Mimi Khalvati for models.

To make it easier still, you can model your ghazal on the free-verse form developed by Adrienne Rich and others in the USA, although the Kashmiri-American poet Agha Shahid Ali wrote of these (1990) that "the form has really been utterly misunderstood in America with these free-verse ghazals. I mean, that's just not the ghazal".

2. What *is* a 'prose poem'? At first glance it doesn't look like a poem at all. It doesn't have the line-breaks of a poem. Printed as prose, it may be a paragraph or so in length, or perhaps have several paragraphs ('stanzas'), and may (or may not) be both right and left justified, and may (or may not) be laid out with more-narrowed-than-usual margins on the page. But aren't line-breaks essential to what makes a poem a poem? No, not

necessarily. By surrendering that most valuable tool, the poet gains access in return to a broader range of syntax and sentence structures. Prose poems are particularly accommodating to poems with a strong narrative line, or a lot of landscape detail – a lot of hard-to-digest data.

Although a prose poem is prose-looking, it features the charged language normally associated with and characteristic of poetry, exploiting linguistic resources such as compression, poetic imagery, cadence, fragmentation, non-literal language, rhythms, figures of speech, rhyme, internal rhyme, assonance, consonance. When you read it, you will hear it breaking some of the normal rules of prose discourse, in order to achieve heightened imagery or emotional effect.

The form is most often traced to nineteenth century French symbolist writers (Rimbaud, Max Jacob, Baudelaire). Prose poetry quickly spread to innovative literary circles in other countries: see examples by Rilke, Kafka, Pablo Neruda, and William Carlos Williams. A post-war American practitioner was Frank O'Hara. For a contemporary American example see Charles Simic.

The above information is mostly lifted from the hand-outs of Ian Seed's prose poetry workshop (with Ian's permission).

Naked Eye Publishing

A fresh approach

As a not-for-profit publisher, Naked Eye is part of the revolution. Co-existing on the newly-levelled playing field alongside the publishing multi-nationals, we prioritise literary and artistic interest. Our books are by and for creatives, intellectuals, art-lovers and bookworms - and at an affordable price. We also publish, where feasible, downloadable versions. Writers we publish do not need agents, nor do they have to financially invest, and they benefit from free global availability and distribution through our printing firm's worldwide partnerships which include Barnes and Noble, Bertrams, Gardners, Waterstones and Amazon. Using the most up-to-date print technology we publish beautiful books of old-fashioned quality.

Our current remit covers world contemporary literary fiction and poetry including new English translations; also art, photography, and our Potted Thesis series: academic theses abridged and retold in a lay-person's terms.

nakedeyepublishing.co.uk

www.ingramcontent.com/pod-product-compliance
Lightning Source LLC
Chambersburg PA
CBHW071323080526
44587CB00018B/3332